A Child's Introduction to Torah

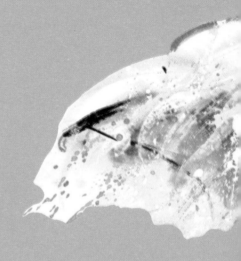

BY SHIRLEY NEWMAN

Edited by Louis Newman

JOSEPH J. SCHWAB, CONSULTANT

Illustrated by Jessica Zemsky

A Child's Introduction to Torah

published by Behrman House, Inc.
for THE MELTON RESEARCH CENTER OF
THE JEWISH THEOLOGICAL SEMINARY OF AMERICA, New York, N.Y.

To the teacher:

The *Teacher's Guide* to this book is a resource to enhance your own knowledge and skill. It contains overviews of Biblical background and specifies the important ideas of each story. The *Guide* anticipates the students' most challenging questions, and includes discussion aids as well as suggestions for class activities. It should be most valuable to lesson preparation.

Contents

To my father,
Joseph Shulman,
who bound me
to the Jewish people
with bonds of love

1

The Gift of Wonder

How can a fly walk on the ceiling without falling off?

What are clouds made of?

When does a seed grow into a tree?

Have *you* ever wondered about such things? Have *you* ever asked such questions?

You probably have, because almost *everybody* wonders about the world and how it "works."

In fact people have thought about such things for as long as there have been human beings on Earth. And how did they try to find answers? They looked. They listened. They touched. They tasted. They smelled. They examined.

That is how they learned that a fly doesn't fall from the ceiling because it has sticky pads on its small feet.

And clouds in the sky are made of thousands and thousands of tiny drops of water.

And seeds begin to grow when they soak up enough water to break their covers.

But there are other questions that cannot be answered by looking, or listening, or touching, or tasting, or smelling, or examining.

Questions about how everything began:

Who started the world that we see around us?

Who designed the seeds so they could grow into plants?

Who taught the birds to fly high in the air?

Who taught the fish to swim deep in the water?

Who?

Have you ever asked questions *like these?* Most people have.

Way, way back, a very long time ago, people wondered about such things, too.

Who made the sky and the water?

Who made the birds and the fish?

And then they believed they found the answers!

"We know," they said. Powerful creatures

called gods made everything around us! Gods that looked like animals. Man-gods, lady-gods, war-gods, all sorts of gods! They told about these gods in exciting and sometimes frightening stories.

The first Jewish people also wondered about the world. They also asked, "How did it all begin?" And, in time, they too found an answer.

But their answer was different from the answers of the other people.

"One God made the earth and the sky and everything there is," was their answer.

"What does God look like?" some wanted to know.

Their teachers said:

"He is not a person. He is not an animal. He is not a thing that we see. He doesn't look like anything."

"And who made God?"

"Nobody made God. We don't know how He came to be."

Still, the people wondered and thought. They kept asking questions about how the world, and everything in it, was made. But that wasn't *all* they wanted to know. Another question puzzled them. How did the Jewish people come to be?

Their teachers knew that these were the questions people *should* ask. For they knew that only man has the gift of wonder—and it was right and good to wonder about oneself, about God and about the world.

They answered the people with many stories.

We find the most important Jewish answers in the Torah. That is why Jewish people study the Torah over and over again—as long as they live.

2

The Creation of the World

The Torah's first story

When God began to create the heaven and the earth, darkness and emptiness were everywhere. And a wind from God blew over the blackness of deep waters.

God said, "Let there be light," and there was light.

God saw that the light was good, and God separated the light from the darkness.

God called the light Day, and the darkness He called Night.

And there was evening
and there was morning,
making one day.

God said, "Let there be a *rakia* in the middle of the waters that it may separate the waters below from the waters above."

God made the *rakia* and separated the waters. God called the *rakia* Sky.

And there was evening
and there was morning,
a second day.

God said, "Let the water below the sky come together in one place, so that the dry land may be seen."

And it was so.

God called the dry land Earth, and the waters that had come together He called Seas.

God saw that this was good.

And God said, "Let the earth send forth growing things: seed-bearing plants and fruit trees of every kind, that bear fruit with seed in it."

And it was so.

The earth brought forth growing things and fruit trees of every kind that bear fruit with seed in it.

And God saw that this was good.

And there was evening
and there was morning,
a third day.

God said, "Let there be lights in the sky, to separate day from night. And they shall mark off the days and the years. And they shall serve as lights in the sky to shine upon the earth."

And it was so.

God made the two great lights—the greater light to rule the day and the smaller light to rule the night. And He made the stars.

And God put the lights in the sky to shine upon the earth; to rule by day and by night, and to separate light from darkness.

God saw that this was good.

And there was evening

and there was morning,

a fourth day.

God said, "Let the waters give forth very many living things, and let birds fly over the earth under the sky."

And God created the great sea monsters, and many kinds of living creatures that creep. These the waters gave forth in large numbers. And God created winged birds of every kind.

God saw that this was good.

God blessed all His creatures and said, "Be fruitful and increase your numbers. Fill up the waters of the sea and let the birds increase over the land."

And there was evening

and there was morning,

a fifth day.

God said, "Let the earth give forth different kinds of living things; cattle, creeping things, and wild animals of every kind."

God made wild animals and cattle of every kind and creeping things of every kind.

And God saw how good this was.

And God said, "I will make man in My image, after My likeness."

AND GOD CREATED MAN IN HIS IMAGE—

IN THE IMAGE OF GOD HE CREATED HIM.

Male and female He created them.

God blessed them and said to them, "Be fruitful and increase. Fill the earth and bring it under your power. Rule the fish of the sea, the birds of the sky and all the living things that creep on earth."

God said, "See, I give you every seed-bearing plant that is upon the earth, and every tree that has seed-bearing fruit. *They shall be yours to eat.* And to all the animals on land, and to everything that creeps on earth, and to all the birds of the sky, I also give all the green plants for food."

And it was so.

God saw all that He had made and found it very good.

And there was evening
and there was morning,
the sixth day.

The heaven and the earth with all their parts were finished.

On the seventh day God finished the work which He had been doing.

He stopped on the seventh day from all the work which He had been doing.

God made the seventh day a special day, different from the six days.

He blessed the seventh day and made it holy.

He did this because on this day all creation stopped.

Such is the story of heaven and earth as they were created.

Today people often ask:

Did things happen just like the Torah says they did in this story?

Didn't it take a very long time, millions and millions of years, for the earth to form?

Why does the Torah say that the sky came from the middle of the waters?

Or that God created the world in six days?

Here is the answer:

Although we now believe that it took much longer than six days for the world to become like the Torah describes it, this first story about God's creating the world in six days is still very dear to us.

Why?

אָדָם

שׁוּתָּפוּ

שֶׁל

הקב"ה

Because the Torah is telling us something very important in a story-way. It is saying:

There is only one God and He made this world and everything in it.

This is the most important thing Jews learn from the Torah.

This means that God made it possible for the world to be—even if it took millions of years and not just six days.

This means that God made it possible for the sky and the sun and the moon and the stars to be—even if He didn't create them just as the story says.

And there is something else that makes the story very important. The Torah says something that people need to hear over and over again. It's very simple.

This world, and the people in it, can be good. But people must help God to make it good.

3

Abraham, the First Jew

Long, long ago—

Before George Washington was the first president—

And before the Pilgrims had the first Thanksgiving day—

And even before Judah Maccabee and the first Hanukkah, a boy named Abraham lived in a place called Ur. This was Abraham of the Torah, Abraham, *the first Jew*.

Ur was a busy city. On ordinary days, the grown-ups did their work, and took care of their families. Children played and helped with the chores. Some went to school, and studied very hard. But on holidays, all work stopped.

The people put on their best clothes, and went to the great temples to pray to their gods.

The people of Ur believed that there were *many* gods. They believed that there was a god to do each separate job in the world.

One god who looked after the rivers.
A different god who took care of the earth.
Another, who was the god of fire.
A god of rain.
A god of growing things.
And on, and on.

Their prayers probably sounded something like this:

"Oh, the god who takes care of the sun,
and keeps it shining each day,
please take care of us, too."

"Oh, the god who protects the moon,
and makes it brighten the sky each night,
please keep us safe also."

"Oh, the god who brings down the rain
from the sky,
please soak our fields so that the grain
will grow tall and thick."

"But Jews don't pray to many gods. Jews believe there is only one God in all the world," you may be saying to yourself. "So how could Abraham, the first Jew, have been part of this city of many gods?"

But Abraham wasn't born a Jew. When he was a boy, he probably prayed to the gods of Ur, like his friends and relatives did.

When did he stop? And how did he come to believe there is only *one God?* How did he become a Jew? We don't know exactly.

In fact, the Torah hardly tells us anything about Abraham's life before he was *seventy-five years old.* By that time, he no longer prayed to the gods of Ur.

About the younger Abraham, it tells us only where he lived, the names of some of his relatives, and that for a long time he and his wife had no children. And nothing about Abraham and the gods, not a word.

"Then how do you know that the people of Ur really prayed to many gods? Maybe they never did," you may ask. "Maybe Abraham never did either."

There is a reason for saying these things about Ur and Abraham.

Nowadays, there are scientists who try to learn how people of long ago lived. We call them archeologists [ar-kee-ah-lo-gists]. They begin their work by digging under the ground and finding things that have been covered by earth for thousands of years.

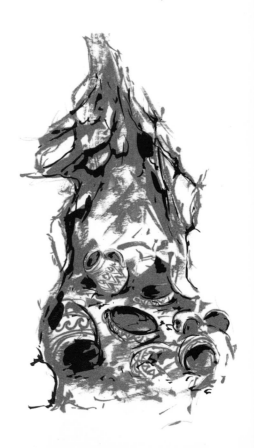

Not too long ago, archeologists discovered the place where the old city of Ur used to be. They were interested in Ur because the Torah says that Abraham's family lived there.

They dug deep under the ground to see if anything from that city might still be buried there. The diggers were very lucky. They found many things.

Among the discoveries were many clay tablets with writing on them. The archeologists learned how to read these tablets. In some they found letters and school lessons. Others had the words of prayers engraved on them. And a few told stories about gods. These findings helped them guess how the people of Ur lived when Abraham was a boy.

But even these don't tell how Abraham became a Jew. Yet we want to know: How did Abraham begin to believe in God? Today we do not have a correct answer to this question. The best we can do is *imagine what may have happened.* We can read all that the Torah tells about Abraham and his family. We can think about the things the archeologists discovered in Ur. Then we can try to imagine some other things that *might* have happened in Abraham's life. Then we can make up a story.

We call such a story a "history-legend." It's a legend because it is a story that has been made up. It is history because it is about real people or real things.

All nations have history-legends about their great leaders. Americans have history-legends about George Washington, Abraham Lincoln and heroes of the Wild West.

The Jewish people have very many history-legends. Some are in the Torah. Wise Jewish teachers told these stories to grown-ups and children.

4

Abraham, the Boy Who Wondered

PART ONE

A History-Legend

One day, the people of Ur were celebrating a great holiday—The Festival of the New Moon.

The buildings were decorated with flowers, and musicians marched through the streets, singing and playing their instruments.

Abraham's house was full of excitement. "I can't find my other sandal," yelled his big brother. "How can I ever get dressed on time?"

"There it is, near the door," his mother told him. "Hurry, we mustn't be late."

After more shouting and rushing, the family was ready. They all looked beautiful as they stepped out into the sunshine. Abraham and his brothers wore their new striped gowns. Their mother and father wore their long, white holiday robes.

"Don't run too far ahead. We don't want to lose you in the crowd," Abraham's father, Terah, called after his three sons.

24

"Don't worry," the boys shouted back, as they skipped and jumped ahead of their parents. "We'll meet you at the big gate outside the temple."

"They'll be safe," whispered Abraham's mother to Terah. "You forget how grown-up they are."

When the parents reached the temple of the moon-god, the boys were waiting inside the gate.

The family was lucky today. Thanks to everyone's hurrying, they had come early enough to find a place right in front of the huge stone statue of the god. "How strong the moon-god is," Terah whispered to his sons.

Then, he handed Abraham a brown clay bowl he had carried from home. "Abraham, today it is *your* turn to put the bowl of wheat flour at the feet of the moon-god's statue. Tell the god we have brought a gift to his temple, and ask him to watch over us."

Abraham knew just what to do. Quickly, he got down on his knees. He placed the bowl before the statue. Then, he bowed low until his forehead touched the ground.

"Oh, great and powerful moon-god, you who are stronger than all the other gods," he prayed, "we hope our gift pleases you. We beg you to keep us safe and healthy."

As Abraham got ready to move back, he did

something strange. He lifted his head and stared. He stared at the stone statue before which he had just placed the bowl of flour.

He looked at the head, with its beautiful head-dress—at the eyes, the nose, the mouth, the beard, all carved so perfectly out of stone—at the clothes with their folds—at the great hands resting the statue's lap—at the feet with their enormous toes.

His eyes kept moving up and down—back and forth. Over and over again, he gazed at every part of the statue. As he looked, all kinds of questions began tumbling about in his head.

"This god of the moon—what *does* he look like? Is he huge and strong like his statue? Does he look like a man—like a king, maybe? Can he hear me when I pray to him? Does he care about me? *Can he really take care of us?*"

"Get up, son," Abraham's mother said gently. "We must make room for the others."

Slowly, still staring at the statue, Abraham rose to his feet.

"What's wrong, child?" his father asked. "You look so strange."

"I-I-I don't know," Abraham stammered. "I-I want to go home!"

Without another word, he spun around and ran from the moon-god's temple.

"I must stop! I must stop thinking about such things—I must!" he kept saying to himself. "It's not good to wonder about the gods. They will be angry. They will hurt me!"

But Abraham couldn't stop wondering about the gods. Day after day, his questions troubled him.

"What do the gods look like? Do they play? Do they eat? Do they fight, as people say they do? Are they really strong—strong enough to do anything they want?"

Again, and again, the questions kept coming back. There was no way to stop them! And Abraham had no answers.

Afraid and unhappy, he made up his mind to ask older and wiser people for help. Perhaps *they* knew answers that would quiet his mind— that would send those questions away forever.

"Father," he asked Terah, "what do the gods look like?"

"Look like?" Terah asked in surprise. "Why, like people, of course. Everyone knows that!"

"How do you know? Have you ever seen them?"

This time Terah sounded angry.

"No, I've never seen them. Nobody has. But I just *know* they look like people. Now go outside, and do your work, and stop asking so many questions. You'll anger the gods, and they will bring troubles on all of us."

Abraham walked outside. But he didn't stop asking.

"Sir," he said to his teacher the next day, "do the gods really argue and fight as people say they do?"

"Of course, Abraham. Everyone knows that."

"And do they care about people? Do they want to protect us?"

"Abraham, you have forgotten what our wise men teach us. *People were made to do the work the gods hate doing*—to dig, to plant, to water, to harvest. We are the *servants* of the gods. I don't know if they care about us. But they need us—just as we free men need slaves."

"Thank you, sir," Abraham said quietly. But still, the thoughts and questions did not stop.

"If the gods quarrel and fight with each other, some of them might get hurt, or even killed. Then, dangerous things could happen in the world. If harm came to the sun-god, maybe the sun would never shine again. And everything would get so cold! Or if the god-of-growing-things were hurt, the crops might not ripen. Then everyone would go hungry!"

The more Abraham wondered, the more mixed up he became.

After a while, he stopped asking older people for answers. They acted so scared when he did, and they always scolded him.

"Don't ask about the gods. You will anger them, and they will bring harm upon us!"

5

Abraham, the Boy Who Wondered

PART TWO

A History-Legend

The months and years passed. Abraham grew to be a young man. He became a shepherd for his father's flocks.

Now, he spent most of his days in the pastures outside the city of Ur. Often, he was alone— just he and the animals.

Sometimes, he even slept outdoors. He loved to lie on the ground, wrapped in the great sheepskin blanket his mother had made.

He loved to look up at the sky at night. He watched the moon as it rose, moved across the blackness, and disappeared into the new morning.

He saw the stars as they changed position. He enjoyed the pinks, and greens, and yellows of the sunrise that *always* followed the night.

Always! Always there was night—and always there was morning. And always there was night —and always there was morning.

He loved the flowers and the grasses of the fields—the pale greens of the cooler months, and the darker greens of the warmer months.

Each month brought its own growing things. There was a month of blue flowers—a month of purple flowers—and a month of red berries that hid among the blades of grass.

Always—always there were changes.

Always one growing thing followed another. And always there was an end, and then a new beginning. And things started to follow one another again, *in the very same order as before.* Pale greens and darker greens—blue flowers and purple flowers.

Slowly, new thoughts began to stir in Abraham's mind. "For all things in heaven and on earth, there seems to be a time and a place. *Everything has its order.*"

"Who made this order? Who watches over it? Who makes sure that the sun doesn't suddenly shine in the black of night—or the moon rise in the bright day? Who keeps the stars from getting scrambled? And the flowers from changing their months?"

Then, an answer pushed its way into Abraham's thoughts. He tried not to think it, but it stayed.

"It cannot be the angry, quarreling gods who keep the world in its order. Somewhere, there must be a god who does not fight with others. There must be a *great god who made everything there is, and watches over the things he made!*"

Abraham looked around. Would the gods hurt him now?

But nothing disturbed the stillness. And the thoughts kept coming.

"I don't think this god looks like a man—not even like a giant man. He is so great. I cannot imagine how he looks, at all."

Finally came the most fearful thought of all. Abraham's heart pounded like a hammer! For a few moments he could not move. *"There are no other gods! I believe there is only one God in all the world!"*

Abraham closed his eyes. The tears rolled slowly down his cheeks. Then, for the first time in many years, he felt happy.

6

There is One Master

A History-Legend

The Rabbis of long ago also wondered about Abraham. What was he like when he was a boy?

How did he learn to believe that there is only one god in all the world?

They knew he was a most unusual man and they created many legends about him.

Here is one:

Ages and ages ago, in a land called Babylon, there was a cruel and mighty king named Nimrod.

"I am a god!" Nimrod said.

"Nimrod is a god," the people repeated. And they bowed low before him.

One morning, Nimrod's magicians walked into the throne room. "Oh, great and mighty king," they cried, "we bring you important news."

"Tell me," Nimrod commanded.

"Early this day, a baby boy was born to your servant, Terah, and his wife. We have learned

that when this baby grows to be a man, he will call out to all who will listen, *'Nimrod is not a god!'*"

Nimrod looked sharply at the faces before him. No sound came from his mouth. No muscle stirred in his body. Only his fingers moved. They closed tightly around the golden arms of the throne chair.

Then, his lips formed a cruel smile. "That will never happen," he said. "Go to Terah and tell him *this:*

'Terah, servant of the great king Nimrod, hear the king's words. We have learned, through our magic, that someday your new son will bring trouble to our land. And so we order you to give us the baby immediately. *He must be killed this very day!*

'But do not be unhappy, Terah. King Nimrod's heart is full of love for you. He will not take your child for nothing. No! He will pay you a bagful of gold as soon as the child is dead!'"

When Terah heard Nimrod's message, he turned pale and cold. Standing in the doorway of his house, he said, "Tell our great king Nimrod that I cannot do as he asks. The baby he wants died soon after it was born."

The moment the messengers were gone, Terah dashed into the house.

"Listen to me, wife," he said in a low voice. Then he told the baby's mother all that had happened.

When Terah finished speaking, it was very still in the house. Only the sound of breathing could be heard. Then came whispering, and, finally, the sounds of quick movements.

Soon, the baby was lying in a small box, covered with cloths of many colors.

"Can he breathe?" Terah's wife asked in a worried voice.

"He's fine," answered Terah, as he picked up the box and walked toward the door.

"Be careful," said the baby's mother softly.

Terah nodded, and stepped outside. After a quick look around, he began to run as fast as he could.

When he reached the edge of the city he stopped to catch his breath. But not for long.

In a few moments he started to run again. This time, he didn't stop until he came to a very big rock. Hidden behind the rock was a deep cave.

Terah slipped through the narrow opening. He stepped into the cave, holding the box with the sleeping baby. Gently he put it down in a dark corner.

"May the gods be good to you and protect you," he said tearfully. "I must leave you now."

The baby, whose name was Abraham, lived in that cave for three long years.

It was a time of strange and surprising happenings. Each morning, when Abraham awoke, he found milk and honey prepared for his meal. With no help at all, he ate and drank until he was full.

When Abraham was only a few days old, he learned to walk. And by the time he was three, he knew how to think and talk like a man.

"The time has come for me to leave this cave," three-year-old Abraham said to himself one day. So he stepped out of his dark home of gray stone. He found himself in the bright world.

And then he wanted to run back! "Where are the walls? Where is the ceiling? Where are all the rocks and cracks that I know so well?"

But he stayed. And things he had never known before began to come to him.

Through his eyes, came the colors of the world. Through his ears, came the sounds of the world. And through his nose, came the smells of the world.

"Who made all this?" Abraham asked in wonder.

"And who made me?" he added.

Quickly his eyes jumped from shape to shape, and from color to color: grays, browns, greens, yellows, rounds, squares, lines, curves.

Then he raised his head, and met the sun. Blinded for a moment, Abraham lowered his eyes and said, "Now I know. This great light made everything there is!"

All that day Abraham prayed to the sun and bowed down before it!

Toward evening, the heavens began to change. Like a proud, handsome king, the yellow moon appeared. And the sun moved away. Soon it was gone.

Abraham breathed deeply. "The light that went away—*that* did *not* make everything there is. No—it is *this* light—the one that chased the other off—it is *this* light that is the maker and the master of all the world!"

All that night, Abraham prayed to the moon and bowed before *it*.

But toward morning, the heavens began to change again. Now it was the *moon* that slipped away *from the burning sun*.

And Abraham knew he had been wrong both times. "*Neither* of these great lights made the things around me," he said. "And neither one made me. There must be another, a master, greater than both of these, who made everything there is. To *him* I will pray, and before *him* I will bow down!"

7

Abraham, the Young Teacher

A History-Legend

One morning, Abraham's father, Terah, said to him, "Son, I feel very tired today. Will you work in the idol shop in my place?"

"I shall be glad to help you, father," Abraham answered. He left the house and walked toward the shop.

Once inside, he stopped and looked around. Everywhere were idols—large ones, small ones, ugly ones and pretty ones. Some stood on the floor, others rested on the shelves. Since no customers had arrived yet, Abraham busied himself dusting and arranging the idols.

"This little stone one looks better over there," he said, "and that tall wooden one must be moved because it is hiding the short ones behind it."

He worked for a long time. And still no customers came. "Perhaps nobody wants to buy an

idol today," Abraham thought. "Soon, it will be time to close the shop, and I will have to tell father that I earned no money at all."

Just then, the shop door squeaked. Into the shop walked a poor, tired old woman. "I have no money to buy an idol-god," she told Abraham.

"But I did bring a present. Please give it to the gods for me, and ask them to protect me and keep me well."

Abraham felt sorry for the tired old woman. "I will do as you ask," he said.

"Thank you," the woman answered, and handed him a bowl of fine, white flour. Then she bowed toward the idols and walked out of the shop.

As soon as the woman was gone, Abraham placed the flour in front of the largest idol in the shop. "Please protect the poor old woman," he prayed. "Please keep her . . ."

Abraham never finished his prayer for the woman. Instead, he stepped back and glanced around at the idols—just as he had done that morning. Only this time his face became pale. His eyes were narrow and drawn tight at the corners. His lips moved—making words without sounds.

Then it happened!

Abraham dashed over to the wood-pile and grabbed a large stick. Then he ran through the

shop, hitting the idols with all his might! Knock! Bang! Crash! Smack!

When he stopped, *there was only one idol left* in the shop that was not broken. It was the largest one, before whom Abraham had placed the flour.

All the rest lay on the floor, their smashed pieces mixed up in piles! Here was the pretty head of a lady-idol. It had landed on the neck of a fat, round-bellied man-idol. There, the hand of a young boy-idol had flown across the room. It was about to tickle the nose of an angry-faced man-idol.

Abraham looked around once more. Then, he walked over to the big idol that was not smashed. Carefully he tucked the stick under its large, wooden arm.

At that moment, the shop door squeaked a second time.

In walked Terah! "Wh-wh-what happened?" Terah stammered, rubbing his eyes to make sure they were not playing tricks on him.

"A very strange thing," Abraham answered quietly. "A woman brought a gift of food for the idols, and asked me to offer it to them. I placed her gift in front of the largest idol. Then the others began to fight and shout. They said that they, too, wanted some of the food."

Terah's face grew redder and redder.

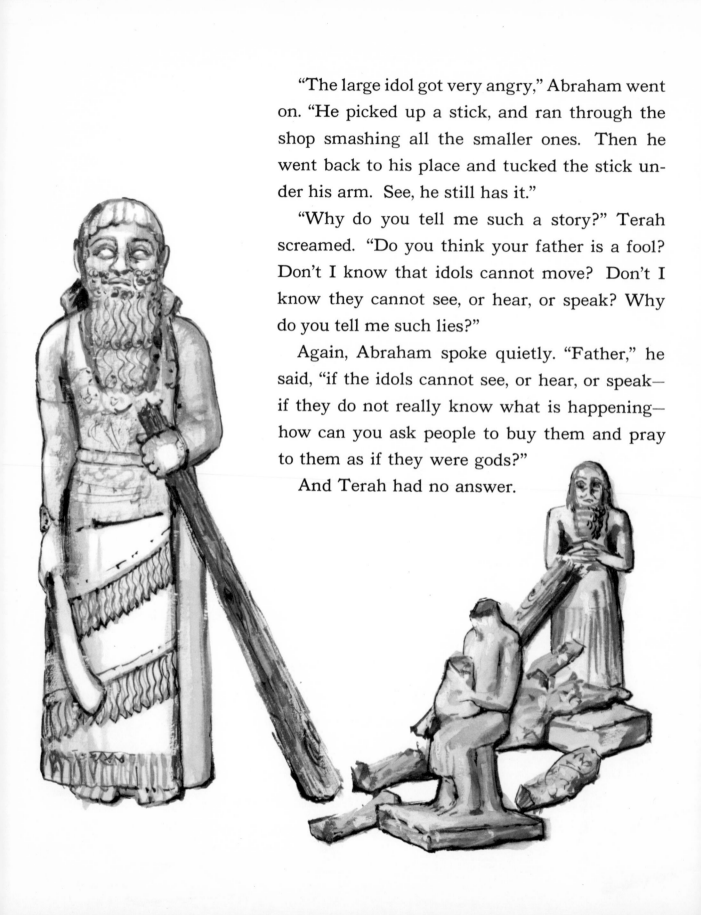

"The large idol got very angry," Abraham went on. "He picked up a stick, and ran through the shop smashing all the smaller ones. Then he went back to his place and tucked the stick under his arm. See, he still has it."

"Why do you tell me such a story?" Terah screamed. "Do you think your father is a fool? Don't I know that idols cannot move? Don't I know they cannot see, or hear, or speak? Why do you tell me such lies?"

Again, Abraham spoke quietly. "Father," he said, "if the idols cannot see, or hear, or speak— if they do not really know what is happening— how can you ask people to buy them and pray to them as if they were gods?"

And Terah had no answer.

8

Abraham Goes to Canaan

The Torah tells us that Abraham lived with his father, Terah, and his two brothers, in the city of Ur.

One of his brothers died, leaving behind a young son named Lot.

Abraham took as his wife a beautiful woman named Sarah. He and Sarah had no children.

One day, Terah, Abraham, Abraham's wife, Sarah, and his nephew, Lot, left Ur. They traveled to a town called Haran, and settled there.

And it happened that when Abraham was seventy-five years old, God said to him:

"You must leave your land, and your father's house, and go to the land that I will show you!"

To leave his land and his father's house!

To go away from his family and his friends! From the wells that gave him water, and the fields that gave him food! How hard that was! How terribly hard!

But Abraham did as God commanded.

He took his wife, Sarah, and his brother's son, Lot, and everything he owned, and the people who helped tend his fields and animals, and set out for the land that God would show him.

It was a long, hard trip. Some days the sun burned like fire, and there was no shade in which to hide. Some nights the wind blew cold, and the animals shivered and huddled together for warmth. But Abraham and his people kept moving on.

At last they came to the land of Canaan, the place we now call Israel. They traveled through the land from north to south.

Then, God spoke to Abraham a second time. "Abraham, this land of Canaan that you have seen—some day it will belong to your children's children's children, and all their children after them."

And Abraham thanked God for bringing him safely to Canaan.

Abraham loved the land of Canaan. He lived first in one place, then another. Everywhere he went, he thanked God for having brought him to Canaan.

Now Abraham grew rich. He had flocks of sheep, herds of cattle, and many tents. He had gold and silver.

"Abraham has everything he wants," people thought.

Yes, he had everything—except what he wanted most of all. Abraham had no child of his own! He and Sarah had only their nephew Lot, the boy they had brought from Haran.

9

Abraham Seeks Peace

Lot grew to be a man. He, too, became rich in tents and flocks.

Soon, there was not enough grass to feed Abraham's animals and Lot's animals in the same fields.

The shepherds who took care of Abraham's animals, and the shepherds who took care of Lot's animals began to fight with each other.

"Lot," said Abraham, "let there not be arguments between you and me, or between my herdsmen and yours. Maybe it is not good for us to live together any longer. Come, stand beside me on this hill, and look around. Then, choose where each of us should go.

"If you go north, I will go south. If you go south, I will go north. You may be the one to decide."

Lot turned his head from side to side and looked and looked. "I will go there, uncle," he said, pointing to the place he wanted.

"Those are the greenest fields," he thought to himself. "I will take the best for myself."

"Go, and be happy, my nephew," Abraham said. And each man went his own way.

Lot went to live near a city named Sodom, and Abraham remained in the land of Canaan.

One morning, many months later, Abraham heard running feet. He looked up and saw a stranger dashing toward his tent.

"Abraham," panted the man, "your nephew, Lot—he's a prisoner. Some kings—from far away —they came and took Lot—and all the people of Sodom—all except the king!"

Then the runner fell down to the ground to rest.

When Abraham heard the news of Lot's capture, he called his servants and his friends together. They set out to try to save Lot and the people of Sodom.

In the middle of the night, they crept up to the camp where the prisoners were kept. Everything was quiet. Even the guards were asleep. Then, making hardly a sound, Abraham and his men attacked the camp. They rescued Lot and the people of Sodom!

When the king of Sodom heard what had happened, he came to meet Abraham. "Take all the riches you have captured," said the king. "Give me back only the people of my city."

But Abraham said to the king of Sodom, "I will not take anything at all from the riches we have captured—not even as much as a thread or a sandal strap!

"For if I do, I fear you may say, 'It is *I* who made Abraham rich!' You should know, O king of Sodom, that only God can make me rich! So I gladly return to you your people and all that belongs to them. Now, go home to your city. And peace be with you."

And Lot also went back to live in Sodom.

After he had saved his nephew, Lot, Abraham returned to the fields and the animals and the people he loved.

Often, as he walked alone among his sheep and goats, he thought to himself sadly, "How I wish I had a child—someone precious to love and to teach."

Then God spoke to Abraham again:

"Abraham, some day the land of Canaan will belong to your children's children's children. Abraham, I will give you and Sarah a son!"

Abraham trembled a little, "God is making me a promise," he whispered.

And God called to Abraham again and said, "Look toward heaven and count the stars if you can." Then He added, "Your offspring shall be as many as the stars!"

10

Abraham Pleads for the Innocent

Some time later, Abraham was sitting at the opening of his tent, looking out. The sun burned overhead and the air was thick with heat. Nothing moved, not even a leaf.

Suddenly, Abraham saw three men standing nearby. He was surprised. "No one should be out in this heat," he thought. Quickly, he stood up and ran to greet the strangers.

"Sirs, if you please, do not go any farther," Abraham said to them. "You must be tired and hot. Let me bring some water so you can bathe your feet. Then, go and rest in the shade of a tree while I prepare a bit of food. After you have eaten, you will go on your way."

"Thank you," the men answered. "Do as you have said."

Abraham hurried into the tent, to his wife Sarah. "Quick, take three cups of our best flour and bake some cakes," he ordered.

Next, Abraham sent for a servant. "Prepare some meat for our guests," he said.

When the food was ready, Abraham set it before the men. They ate in silence. After the meal, they asked, "Where is your wife, Sarah?" "There, in the tent," Abraham answered.

And one of the men said, "Soon Sarah will have a son!"

Now, Sarah was listening at the opening of her tent. She laughed to herself, saying, "How foolish! Everyone knows that Abraham and I are much too old to have children!"

When the day grew cooler, the men set out on their way. As they walked, they turned and looked in the direction of Sodom, the city where Lot had gone to live.

As Abraham walked with the men to see them off, God said, "Shall I hide from Abraham what I am about to do? Abraham who will teach his children to walk in My ways by doing what is just and right?"

Then God said to Abraham, "There are two cities, Sodom and Gomorrah, whose people do not live as people should. Day and night I hear the cries of those whom they harm. The voices call to Me and say, 'They steal! They hurt! They kill! They burn! They hate the stranger and do not help the poor!' If everything I hear is true, I shall have to destroy these cities!"

Abraham said nothing. His eyes stared into the distance and sharp stabs of pain seemed to be hurting his face.

At that moment, the three men left. They were messengers of God on their way to Sodom.

Then Abraham stepped forward and said: "My Lord, will You destroy the innocent along with the guilty? What if there are fifty innocent people in Sodom? Should You not forgive the *whole city* because of these fifty? Would it not be *wrong* to destroy the innocent as well as the guilty? You must not do such a thing! You must not destroy the good together with the bad! No, God, You must not do this! Remember, You are the great judge of the world! Should not the Judge of all the earth act justly?"

And God answered, "If I find within the city of Sodom fifty innocent ones, I will forgive the whole place because of them."

Abraham spoke again. "Here I dare to speak to the Lord—I, who am but dust and ashes. But what if there should be five missing from the fifty? Will You destroy the whole city because five are missing?"

And God said, "I will not destroy it if I find forty-five there."

Then Abraham spoke again. "What if forty should be found there?"

God said, "I will not do it for the sake of the forty."

"I hope I will not anger You if I go on speaking, but what if thirty should be found there?"

"I will not do it if I find thirty there."

And Abraham said, "I dare again to speak to the Lord. What if twenty should be found there?"

"I will not destroy for the sake of the twenty."

And Abraham said, "Please do not be angry if I speak just this last time. What if there are ten innocent?"

And God answered, "I will not destroy, for the sake of the ten."

But there were not even ten innocents, and the wicked cities were destroyed.

The next morning, Abraham hurried to the place where he had stood before God. He looked down toward Sodom and Gomorrah. There he saw the smoke from the land rising like the smoke from a great oven. Nothing was left of the cities or their people.

Only Lot and his family did not die. God took special care of Lot because he was Abraham's nephew. And God's messengers brought Lot and his family out of Sodom just before the city was destroyed.

11

Isaac Lives in Canaan

God's promise did come true.

A child was born to Abraham and Sarah! A son of their very own! They called him Isaac.

Isaac was a beautiful child. Sarah loved to look at him as he ran and played in the grass each day.

"It's true. I really have a son!" she said to herself. And joyful smiles lighted her face.

Abraham, too, loved his son. "Come, run into my arms, little one," he laughed when Isaac was learning to take his first steps.

"How strong you are," he told him when Isaac grew old enough to help care for the sheep and goats.

And each day, in many ways, Abraham taught Isaac to know that there is only one God in the world.

Time passed, and Isaac grew to be a man.

Then a sad thing happened—Sarah, Abraham's wife, Isaac's mother, died. Abraham and Isaac were very lonely without her.

"I, too, am old," Abraham thought to himself. "Soon I shall also have to die. Then Isaac will be left alone."

"Eliezer," he called to his servant, "when I came here from far off Haran, you came with me. For many years, you have lived with me and helped me. You love Isaac as much as I do. Now, I must ask a great favor of you. Go back to the land where I was born, and find there a wife for my son. Bring her here, to the land of Canaan."

And Eliezer said to Abraham, "I will do as you ask. But what if the girl I choose will not want to come with me? Shall I then take Isaac back to the land from which you came, and let him marry her there?"

"No," Abraham answered. "God will help you find a wife for Isaac. If the girl will not go with you, then come back alone. But Isaac must never leave the land of Canaan!"

So Eliezer took ten camels, and some men to help him, and started out for the land from which Abraham had come.

The trip took many days, but at last the travelers reached the place they wanted. It was almost nighttime.

"Let us rest near this well," Eliezer said.

Then Eliezer sat on the ground beside his camels and began to whisper.

"O God, I beg You to help me. Soon the girls of the city will come to the well to get water for their families. I will say to one of them: 'Please let me drink from your jug of water.' If she answers: 'Drink, and I will also bring water for your camels,' let her be the girl whom You, God, have sent to become the wife of Isaac."

Eliezer had hardly finished his prayer when a beautiful girl appeared. She went down to the well, filled her jug and came up. Eliezer ran toward her.

"Please let me sip a little water from your jug," he asked.

"Drink as much as you like," she said as she handed him her jug. "Drink, and I will also bring enough for your camels."

Eliezer could hardly believe his ears!

When the camels finished drinking, he reached into his bag and took out a ring and two golden bracelets.

"These gifts are for you," he said, giving them to the girl.

For a few moments, there was silence. Then Eliezer spoke again. "Whose daughter are you?" he asked. "And is there room in your father's house for us to spend the night?"

"I am Rebekah," she told him. "My father's name is Bethuel. There is plenty of straw and feed at home, and also room to spend the night."

"Rebekah, Bethuel," Eliezer thought to himself. "These are the names of people in Abraham's family! God has led me to the home of Abraham's nieces and nephews!"

And he bowed his head low. "Thank You, God," he whispered.

While Eliezer waited beside the well, Rebekah ran home.

Soon, a young man appeared at the well.

"I am Laban, Rebekah's brother," he said. "I have come to show you the way to our house. Your camels will be taken care of while you and your men eat and drink with us."

Eliezer went with Laban. The bags were unloaded, and the camels were given straw and food. Water was brought to bathe the feet of the tired travelers, and food was set before them.

But Eliezer was not ready to eat. "I will not eat until I have told you my tale," he said.

"Speak," said Laban, "and we will listen."

"I am the servant of your father's uncle, Abraham," Eliezer began, "of Abraham who lives in the land of Canaan. God has blessed my master and made him rich. And my master has an only son, Isaac, to whom he has given everything he owns. Now the time has come for Isaac to marry.

"Abraham said to me, 'Isaac must not marry a girl from Canaan. You must go to the land where I was born, to my family, and bring back a wife for my son.'

"I did as Abraham asked. I have traveled for many days. This evening after a tiring day's journey, I arrived in your city, and sat down to rest beside the well.

" 'O God,' I prayed, 'soon the girls will come to the well to get water. I will say to one, "Please let me drink a little water from your jug." If she answers, "You may drink, and I will also bring water for your camels"— let her be the wife you have chosen for my master's son.'

"I had just finished praying, when Rebekah came along.

" 'Please give me a drink,' I said to her. She quickly lowered her jug and said, 'Drink and I will also bring water for your camels.'

" 'Whose daughter are you?' I asked. When she told me who her family was, I could hardly believe my ears! I thanked God who had sent my master's niece as a wife for his son, Isaac.

"Now, I ask you to let Rebekah come back with me to the land of Canaan to marry Abraham's son."

"If Rebekah chooses to go, you may take her with you," answered the girl's family.

"I will go," Rebekah said softly.

And she left her home, and started out for the land of Canaan.

Here she and Isaac were married.

Isaac loved her dearly.

12

Rebekah Tries to Help God

This is the story of Isaac.

For many years after Isaac and Rebekah were married, they had no children. This was a great sadness in their lives.

Then, at last, Rebekah discovered that she was to become a mother. Now, the happiness of Isaac and Rebekah was complete!

But all was not well.

When it was almost time for her children to be born, Rebekah felt that twins were fighting within her.

Rebekah was troubled and asked of God, "If the children are already fighting, what is the use of my life?"

God explained to her, "You are about to give birth to *two sons*. Their fighting means that when they grow to be men, the younger—not the older—will become head of the family!"

And so it was that Isaac and Rebekah became

parents of twins—two boys, who did not look one bit alike!

The first-born was red, with hairy arms and legs. He was called Esau.

The second was fair and smooth-skinned. He was Jacob.

When the boys grew up, Esau became a hunter, while Jacob worked near home. Isaac loved Esau, but Rebekah loved Jacob.

In time, Isaac grew old, and his eyes became weaker and weaker, until he could no longer see.

"Esau," he called to his older son one day.

"Here I am, father," Esau answered.

And Isaac said, "I am so old you see, that I may soon die. Now, go out into the country and hunt me an animal that is good for food. Then, cook the meat so that I may eat it. After that, I will bless you. I will ask God to let you become rich and strong. And you will be the head of the family when I die."

"Thank you, father. I will go now," Esau said, and he left Isaac's tent.

Nearby, Rebekah had been listening. She remembered her secret—God's promise that *Jacob,* not Esau, would one day become the head of the family! She had never told anyone about this promise.

As soon as Esau was gone, Rebekah ran to find Jacob. "I overheard your father speaking to your brother," she said, and told him what Isaac had said to Esau.

"Now, Jacob, listen and do as I say," she said quickly. "Prepare two young goats and I will cook the meat the way your father likes. Then you will pretend to be Esau! You will take the food to your blind father. He will think that you are your brother, and he will bless *you* instead of him."

"But, mother," Jacob argued, "I can't fool my father. Esau is a hairy man, and my arms are smooth. If my father touches me, he will know I am Jacob, and he will be very angry with me for trying to trick him."

"Just do as I say," Rebekah scolded. And Jacob did as she said.

13

Jacob in Danger

Jacob got the goats and brought them to Rebekah. She prepared the meat just as Isaac liked. Then, she took the best clothes of her older son, Esau, and had her younger son, Jacob, put them on.

When he was dressed, she said to him, "Hold out your arms." Without a question, Jacob did as his mother asked. And she covered his outstretched arms with the furry, hairy skins that he had taken off the young goats.

"Now your arms feel as hairy as Esau's. You are ready to take the food into your father's tent."

Jacob picked up the dish and carried it to his father's bedside.

"Father," he said to the blind man. Isaac turned his head toward the voice.

"Which of my sons are you?" he asked.

"I am Esau," Jacob answered. "I have done as

you told me. Please sit up and eat so that you may give me your blessing."

Isaac did not move. "How did you come back so quickly, my son?" he asked.

"Because God helped me," Jacob said.

Isaac reached out toward Jacob. "Come closer so that I may feel you, my son—that I may know whether you are really Esau or not," Isaac said.

Jacob came closer, and Isaac touched him. "The voice is the voice of Jacob, but the hands are the hands of Esau. Are you really my son Esau?"

"I am," Jacob lied.

Then Isaac ate and blessed him. "I pray that God will make you rich and strong, and that *you will become the leader of the family.*"

Isaac leaned back to rest, and Jacob left his father's tent.

At that moment, Esau came home from the hunt. He prepared the meat, and brought it to his father. "Sit up and eat, father, so that you may bless me as you promised."

"Who are you?" Isaac asked.

"I am Esau, your first-born—your son who brings you food from the hunt."

Isaac's body began to tremble. "We have been fooled!" he called out in a terrible voice. "Your

brother pretended to be you. He brought me food, and I blessed *him* instead of *you!*"

When Esau heard his father's words, he burst into bitter sobbing.

"Bless me too, father," he cried. "Have you not a blessing for me, too?"

So Isaac blessed Esau also. But the blessing of Esau was not as good as the blessing of Jacob. Jacob was to become the head of the family!

After that Esau did not speak to Jacob. "I will wait until my father, Isaac, dies," he said to himself. "Then I will kill my brother Jacob for what he did to me!"

"Esau is planning to kill Jacob," someone told Rebekah.

"Oh no!" she moaned, and a choking feeling filled her throat. She knew that she must act very quickly!

She sent for Jacob, and said to him, "Your brother Esau is planning to kill you. Again you must do as I say. Leave here this very day! Go to Haran, to my brother Laban's house. Stay with him until Esau feels less angry. Then, I will send for you. Go quickly. Let me not lose you both in one day!"

That afternoon, Jacob left his family and set out for Haran.

14

Jacob is Tricked

Jacob's trip to Haran took many weeks. It was a time of fear and loneliness. "Will I ever return to my father's house?" he often wondered out loud.

One night, as Jacob slept, his head resting on a stone, he dreamed a dream. And in his dream, God said: "Jacob, some day this land will belong to you, and to all who come after you. Wherever you go I will protect you, and I will bring you back to this land."

Early the next morning, Jacob awoke. Remembering his dream, he made a promise. "If God protects me on this journey, and gives me bread to eat and clothing to wear—then He will be my God, and I shall always bring Him gifts."

A little while later, Jacob set out once more. He traveled until he reached the land of the Easterners. Here, he stopped to rest.

Looking around, he saw a well covered with

a huge stone. Three flocks of sheep were lying beside the well. Nearby stood their shepherds. They were waiting for the rest of the flocks to gather. Then the large stone on the mouth of the well would be rolled off, and all the sheep would be given water.

"My friends, where are you from?" Jacob asked, walking toward the shepherds.

"We are from Haran," they answered.

"Do you know Laban, the son of Nahor?"

"Yes, we do."

"Is he well?" Jacob continued.

"He is," the shepherds said. "And there is his daughter, Rachel, coming with her flock."

When Jacob saw Rachel, the daughter of his mother's brother, and the flock she was shepherding, he went up to the well and rolled the huge stone off by himself! Quickly, he watered her sheep. Then he kissed Rachel and burst into tears.

"I am Jacob—Rebekah's son—your father's nephew," he said to her.

Rachel looked at the stranger. "Rebekah's son?" she questioned.

"Rebekah's son!" she repeated, as she suddenly remembered who Jacob was. And she ran to tell her father.

On hearing the news about his sister's son, Laban ran to greet him. He kissed Jacob, and

took him into his house. Jacob told Laban all that had happened, and he stayed on in Laban's house.

Jacob became a shepherd for Laban's flocks. After a month, Laban said to Jacob, "It is not right that you should work for nothing. Tell me, what shall your wages be?"

Now Laban had two daughters. The name of the older one was Leah, and the name of the younger one was Rachel. Rachel was very beautiful, but Leah was not. Jacob had grown to love Rachel. So when his uncle asked what his wages should be, he answered, "I will work for seven years without wages, if you will let me marry Rachel when that time is up."

"Better that I should give her to you than I should give her to a stranger," said Laban. "Stay with me."

Jacob worked seven years for Rachel, and the time seemed to pass quickly because of his love for her. Then Jacob said to Laban, "My seven years are over. Now give me Rachel as my wife."

"You will be married tonight," Laban answered. And Laban gathered all the people of the place and made a great party. But the bride was nowhere to be seen.

"Where is Rachel?" Jacob asked.

"I will bring her to you when evening comes," Laban said.

A few hours later, Laban stood before the opening of Jacob's tent. "Jacob, I have brought you your wife."

Jacob's heart filled with joy. "Come in my beautiful Rachel," he said.

The night was very dark. Jacob could not even see his new wife's face. But he was pleased to have her with him.

The next morning, as light began to come into the tent, Jacob awoke. Happily, he turned to look at the face of Rachel, who was asleep beside him.

"Oh no!" he called out in a terrible voice. And his whole body began to tremble. "I have been fooled! You are not Rachel whom I love. You are her sister, Leah! How could your father play this trick on me?"

Still trembling, Jacob ran to find Laban. "Why did you fool me?" Jacob screamed.

Laban only smiled and said, "In our country, the older daughter must get married before the younger one. But, after one week, you may marry Rachel also, if you will work for me for seven more years."

Jacob agreed to what Laban said. He married Rachel and worked for seven more years without wages.

15

Jacob Raises a Family

Jacob became the father of many children. His favorite was Joseph, the first of Rachel's two sons.

After the birth of Joseph, Jacob said to Laban, "Give me my wives and my children, for whom I have served you, and let me go back to my own homeland."

But Laban did not want him to leave. "No. Do not go," he said. "I know that God has blessed me on account of you. Stay! I will pay you whatever you ask."

But Jacob said, "Pay me nothing. Just let me go among your animals and take out all the speckled and spotted goats, and the dark-colored sheep. These will become my own flock."

"Good," said Laban.

That very day, Laban secretly removed all the sheep and goats he had promised to Jacob, and sent them far away in the charge of his sons.

But God helped Jacob. The flocks that he

cared for soon gave birth to new lambs and kids. And many of the lambs were dark colored, and many of the baby goats were speckled or spotted. Jacob took these as his wages and he became rich. Soon, he owned large flocks of sheep and goats.

One day, Jacob heard that Laban's sons were saying, "Jacob has taken our father's wealth." He also noticed that Laban was not as friendly to him as he had been before. So Jacob called his wives, Rachel and Leah, to the field. He said to them, "As you know, I have served your father well. But he has cheated me again and again. God, however, would not let him do me harm. He gave me animals from your father's flock. And once, in a dream, God said to me, 'Leave this land and return to the land where you were born.'"

Jacob then took his wives, and his children, and the animals he owned, and the servants who worked for him, and left Haran.

When Laban discovered that Jacob and his family were gone, he decided to chase after him. For seven days, he rode very fast. Finally he caught up with Jacob.

"Why did you run off so secretly?" Laban said. "It was a foolish thing for you to do, because you know I can do you great harm. But I will not hurt you this time because God said to me in a dream last night, 'Do neither good nor bad to Jacob.'"

Now Jacob became very angry. "What wrong have I done that you should chase me this way?" he cried. "For twenty years I served you well—fourteen for your daughters and six for your flocks. Under the burning sun I watched over your animals. And I watched over them in the freezing cold of the night. I protected them always.

"I never took what did not belong to me. When wild animals snatched your sheep or goats, I paid for what you lost. But you—you tried to cheat me again and again. If God had not protected me, you would have taken everything I own."

Then Laban said to Jacob, "Let us agree not to do each other harm from now on."

And Jacob agreed.

Early the next morning, Laban kissed his daughters and grandchildren, and left for home.

16

Esau Forgives Jacob

Jacob, too, went on his way. After many days, he saw that he was not far from the place where his brother Esau now lived.

A great fear rushed over him. "Go ahead of us," Jacob said to some of his servants. "Find Esau and say to him, 'To my master, Esau, this is what your servant, Jacob, says. I stayed with Laban all this time and became rich in cattle and sheep. I send you this message because I hope you will be friendly.'"

The messengers went and came back, saying, "Esau himself is coming to meet you, and there are four hundred men with him."

"O God," Jacob prayed. "I know I do not deserve the kindness You have shown me. Twenty years ago I left my father's house with nothing but my stick and the clothes on my back. You watched over me and kept me from harm. You gave me wives and children. You made me rich.

"Save me now, I beg You, from my brother Esau's anger. I fear he is coming to kill us. Please remember the promise in which You said, 'Jacob, I will be good to you. I will give you children and children's children. Their number will be too great to count—like the grains of sand on the shore of the sea.'"

The next day, Jacob took goats and sheep, camels, cows, bulls, and donkeys.

Again he spoke to his servants. "Take these animals, and go ahead of us. When Esau meets you and asks, 'Where are you going? And whose animals are these?' you are to answer, 'The animals are a gift that your servant, Jacob, is sending to his master, Esau. And Jacob is following behind us.'"

"If I send Esau gifts, maybe he will be kind to me," Jacob thought to himself.

Jacob and his family waited through the night. In the early morning they set out in the direction of Esau. Soon, Jacob saw Esau coming toward him with his four hundred men. Once more, Jacob turned cold with fear. With his head bent low, he walked ahead of his family, bowing seven times, until he reached his brother.

Esau ran forward. He threw his arms around Jacob and kissed him! Both men began to cry.

"Who are these people with you?" Esau asked. "This is the family with which God has blessed me," Jacob answered.

"And why did you send all the servants and animals ahead of you?"

"So that you would be kind to me," Jacob said.

Esau smiled. "I have enough, my brother," he said. "Keep what is yours."

But Jacob begged him, saying, "Please accept my present to you. God has been very good to me and I am rich. I want to share my wealth with you."

When Jacob begged him again and again, Esau finally accepted the gifts.

A short time later, Esau said, "Let us move on. I will travel slowly and go with you."

"Do not trouble yourself, my master," Jacob said. "The children need much care and the nursing animals are very delicate. If they travel too fast for even one day, all the flocks will die. I must therefore move very slowly. I dare not rush the children or the animals."

"Then let me leave some of my men with you, to help you," Esau offered.

"Oh no! My master is too kind to me," Jacob said.

With these words, the brothers parted. Esau returned to his home in Seir, while Jacob traveled on toward Canaan.

Earlier, before Jacob and Esau met, God had appeared to Jacob and said,
"You, whose name is Jacob,
You shall no longer be called Jacob.
Israel shall be your name!"
In a way, Jacob-who-was-now-called-Israel became a new person. He was gentler and sadder than ever before.

When Isaac died of old age, *both* of his sons buried him. And there was no more hate between them.

17

Joseph, the Dreamer

Jacob now lived in the land of Canaan with his twelve sons and one daughter. His favorite son was Joseph. Joseph's mother, Rachel, had died when her younger child, Benjamin, was born.

Joseph worked as a shepherd with his older brothers. Sometimes he told his father that they were not doing things right.

Jacob loved Joseph so much that he made him a special coat—a coat more beautiful than anything his brothers had.

When his brothers saw that their father loved Joseph more than any of them, they were filled with hate.

"Here comes our father's favorite," they said whenever they saw Joseph. And they could not even speak a friendly word to him.

Once, Joseph had a dream which he told to his brothers. He said to them, "Hear this dream that I have dreamed. In it, we were all tying

sheaves in the field. Suddenly, my sheaf stood up straight and tall. Then, your sheaves gathered around, and bowed low to my sheaf."

"Do you think that some day *we* will all bow down to *you?* Do you plan to rule over us?" his brothers asked angrily. And they hated him even more for his talk about his dreams.

One day, Jacob said to Joseph, "Your brothers are near the town of Shechem pasturing our animals. They have been gone for a few days. Go and find them. Then hurry back to let me know if all is well with them and with the flocks."

"I shall be ready to leave in a few minutes," Joseph said. And he ran to put on his beautiful coat.

Joseph walked and walked until he found the place where his brothers were pasturing the animals. Suddenly, some of the brothers noticed him walking toward their camp. "Here comes our father's dreamer," they said. "Let us kill him and throw him into one of the pits in the ground! We can say, 'A wild beast ate him.' Then we will see what comes of his dreams!"

"No," said Reuben, Joseph's oldest brother. "Let us not take his life! Just throw him into the pit and leave him there. But do not kill him with your own hands!"

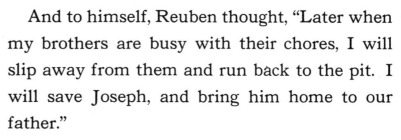

And to himself, Reuben thought, "Later when my brothers are busy with their chores, I will slip away from them and run back to the pit. I will save Joseph, and bring him home to our father."

"Reuben is right," said Joseph's brothers. "We will not shed Joseph's blood."

And they waited.

Joseph walked up to his brothers' camp. "Are you well?" he asked.

His brothers looked at him without a word. "Why don't they answer?" he wondered. "And why are they looking at me like that?"

Suddenly, one of the brothers jumped on Joseph. He pushed him down, and held him on the ground while the others pulled off his beautiful coat. Then, they dragged him to the open pit and threw him in! The pit was empty. There was no water in it.

After this, they sat down to eat a meal.

A short time later, a group of men on camels came riding toward the camp. "Who are you?" one of the brothers called out. "And where are you going?"

"We are traders," the strangers answered, "and we are going down to Egypt to sell the things that are loaded on our camels."

As soon as Judah, another one of Joseph's brothers, heard this, an idea flashed into his mind. "If we leave Joseph in the pit," he said, "he will surely die. Let us not do this to him. After all he is our brother. Instead, let us ask these traveling traders to buy him. They can sell him in Egypt as a slave!"

His brothers agreed. Quickly, they pulled Joseph out of the pit. They sold him to the traders for twenty pieces of silver.

While all this was happening, Reuben was not with his brothers. He had gone to the pasture to check the flocks. On his way back, he passed by Joseph's pit. "Joseph," he called softly, "it is I—Reuben."

There was no answer. "Joseph," he called again, coming closer. Still there was no answer.

He bent over the edge of the pit, and looked in. "Joseph is gone!" he screamed, running to his brothers. "He's not in the pit! What will we tell our father?"

Nobody spoke!

Then a voice broke the stillness. "Let us kill one of our goats and dip Joseph's coat into the blood."

And this is what they did.

The next day, they brought the coat to their

father and said, "We found this in the field. Does it belong to your son?"

Jacob recognized the coat. "A wild animal has eaten Joseph!" he cried. And he fell to the ground sobbing. "I will never see my son again!"

From that day on, Jacob was always sad.

18

Joseph, the Slave

The traders reached Egypt. "Come and see what
we have brought," they called to the people in
the market-place. "Who will buy our delicious
foods? Who will buy our wonderful medicines?
And who will buy a strong, healthy slave boy?"

A man stepped up. He looked at Joseph, and
felt his muscles. "He is strong enough to work,"
the man said to himself.

So he paid the traders, and took Joseph.

The man, whose name was Potiphar, was a
kind master. "Joseph is a fine slave," he said. "I
have never had a better one." Soon, he put
Joseph in charge of his household.

But Potiphar's wife caused trouble for the
tall, handsome young slave. "Let the others do
the work of the household. My husband will
never know," she said to him. "I want you to
stay with me."

Joseph paid no attention to her and went on working, as he knew he should.

One day, Joseph came into the house to do his work. Potiphar's wife grabbed the sleeve of his coat and tried to make him stay. Joseph pulled away, and ran out. But the coat was left in her hands.

She was very angry. "That slave will pay for this!" she said.

As soon as Potiphar came home she told him, "Your wonderful slave works only when people watch him!"

Then, there were more lies. "When nobody is looking, he tries to hide here in the house with me. See, he left his coat today. He is no good—this Hebrew slave of yours."

Potiphar listened. His eyes flashed with anger. "I won't let that slave fool me!" he shouted.

And he threw Joseph into prison and forgot about him.

Not far from the prison stood the palace of Pharaoh, king of Egypt. He had many servants. One of them was a cupbearer who brought Pharaoh his wine each day. Another was a baker who prepared his favorite cakes.

One day the king became angry at the two servants. "Throw them into prison," he commanded.

Grabbing the cupbearer and the baker, the king's guards dragged the men away. They tossed them into a prison cell. It was the very same cell where Joseph was kept.

The three men became good friends.

One morning Joseph noticed that the other two were troubled. "Why do you look so unhappy?" he asked.

"Because we both had dreams last night, and there is nobody to tell us what they mean," they answered.

"Tell them to me," Joseph said. "Perhaps God will help me understand them."

The cupbearer told his dream first.

"This is the meaning of your dream," Joseph said to him. "In three days, Pharaoh will take you out of prison, and bring you back to the palace to work for him. When this happens, I beg you to tell Pharaoh about me. Perhaps he will free me from this place. I have done nothing wrong!"

When the baker heard Joseph's words to the cupbearer, he, too, told his dream. For him, Joseph had sad news. "Your dream means that Pharaoh will put you to death in three days," Joseph said.

And everything that Joseph told the men came true.

But the cupbearer did not remember to tell Pharaoh about Joseph.

19

The Dreams of Pharaoh

Two years passed. Joseph was still in prison.

Then, one night, Pharaoh dreamed a dream. He dreamed he was standing near the Nile river, when out of the water came seven fat and healthy cows. They began to nibble the grass that grew beside the water.

Soon, seven other cows came up from the water. These were thin and ugly cows. They stood beside the fat and healthy cows, opened their mouths, and ate them!

Pharaoh awoke! Then he fell asleep again and he dreamed another dream. He saw a tall stalk. On it grew seven solid and healthy ears of grain. Close behind it, grew a second stalk with seven ears of grain. But these were brown and dry, and not good for eating. And the brown dry grain swallowed up the healthy grain!

Next morning, Pharaoh sent for all the magicians of Egypt. "Tell me what my dreams

mean," he commanded. But nobody could help him.

Suddenly, Pharaoh's cupbearer spoke up. "Your Majesty," he said quietly, "once you were angry with me and had me thrown into prison. There I dreamed a dream that I did not understand. But another prisoner, a Hebrew slave named Joseph, told me the meaning of my dream. And all he said came true."

"Bring me the slave," Pharaoh ordered.

Joseph was rushed to Pharaoh from prison. "Young man," said Pharaoh, "I hear that you understand the meaning of dreams. I have brought you here to help me!"

But Joseph answered Pharaoh and said, "Oh no, your Majesty. *I* cannot understand the meaning of dreams *myself*. Perhaps God will help Pharaoh."

So Pharaoh told Joseph his dreams, and Joseph listened.

Then he said to Pharaoh, "Both dreams mean the same thing. This is their meaning:

"For seven years there will be plenty of food in Egypt—more food than the people can eat. But then the ground will dry up and nothing will grow. For the next seven years the people will go hungry, and they will die because there will not be enough food in the land.

"This is the meaning of your dreams, Oh Pharaoh. God has helped me to understand them."

The throne-room was very quiet.

Then Joseph spoke again. "You can help your people if you do as I say, great king. Find a wise and good man and tell him to talk to the people. Let him ask them to bring him part of each crop of grain that grows in the seven good years. Then have him store that grain carefully so that it will not spoil. In this way, he can save enough food for the seven dry years, and your people will not starve to death!"

Pharaoh leaned forward on his throne.

"Young man," he said, "I choose *you* to do the things you have just spoken of. From this minute on, *you* will be in charge of all the people of Egypt! And everyone will do as you command! You will be the most important man in the land—next to the king himself!"

The seven good years passed, and the seven dry years began—just as Joseph had said they would. Nothing grew in the fields. But nobody in Egypt went hungry. The people came to Joseph and he gave them the food he had stored away.

Then people from other lands also began to come to Egypt for food, because the earth was dry everywhere, and no grain grew. *And Joseph had enough for all who came.*

20

The Dreams Come True

In the land of Canaan, too, there was hunger.

Jacob said to his sons, "I hear there is food to be had in Egypt. Go and bring back as much as your animals can carry, that we may live and not die."

So ten of Joseph's brothers saddled their donkeys, and left to buy food in Egypt. Only Benjamin, the youngest, did not go. Jacob wanted Benjamin to stay with him.

The brothers rode until they reached the city where Joseph was giving out food. Here, they waited their turn to come before the man who had saved Egypt from starvation!

As soon as Joseph saw his brothers he recognized them. But he acted like a stranger, and spoke angrily to them. "Where do you come from?" he asked.

"From the land of Canaan, Oh Great Man of Egypt," they answered. They bowed low with

their faces to the ground. "We have come to buy food for our families."

Joseph remembered the dreams he had dreamed about his brothers! Were they coming true now? "You are lying," Joseph said, pretending not to believe them. "You have no families in Canaan!"

"Please believe us, Oh Great Man," the brothers begged. "We are all sons of one man. We have wives and children and an old father in Canaan. We also have a young brother at home—the youngest son of our father."

"Why do you keep telling me lies?" Joseph screamed. "I know who you are. You are spies! You have come to find out the secrets of Egypt for your king!"

"Please, believe us," the brothers begged again, bowing low before Joseph. "We are not spies. We are Hebrews with hungry families at home. We must bring them food!"

But Joseph refused to listen. "No, you are spies!" he shouted again.

Then his eyes began to move slowly from face to face. "Perhaps you are telling the truth after all," he suddenly said. "By this test I will know. *Nine* of you are to stay here as my prisoners while *one* goes home to bring back your youngest brother. If you do this, I will believe that you are not spies." And he locked them in prison for three days.

On the third day, Joseph said to his brothers, "I want to do what is right, for I fear God. I have, therefore, changed my plan. Only *one* of you will remain in this prison. The others will take food back to your starving families. When this food is gone, you must come back for more, and you must bring me your youngest brother! By this I will know that you are telling the truth. Then I will free the one who I am keeping as my prisoner."

The brothers looked at each other in fright. "Surely this is our punishment for what we did to Joseph so many years ago," they whispered. "For we watched him suffer, and paid no attention when he begged for help."

When Joseph heard their words, he turned away and cried. But he still pretended not to know them. Then he took his brother Simeon prisoner, and told the others to get ready to leave.

The moment the brothers were out of the room, Joseph called his servant and said, "Fill their bags with food. And put each one's money back into his bag."

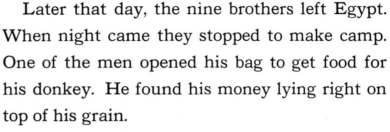

Later that day, the nine brothers left Egypt. When night came they stopped to make camp. One of the men opened his bag to get food for his donkey. He found his money lying right on top of his grain.

"Look, my money has been returned," he said to his brothers. "It is here in my bag!" Trembling, they turned to one another and said, "What is this that God has done to us?"

When the brothers came back to the land of Canaan, they told their father all that had happened in Egypt. Then, as they were emptying their bags, each one found his money hidden in the grain.

"What does this mean?" they asked. But nobody understood.

21

Benjamin in God's Hand

After many weeks, Jacob called his sons together.

"The food you brought from Egypt is almost gone," he said. "You must go back and bring a fresh supply."

"Only if you let Benjamin come with us—" the brothers answered. "The great man of Egypt commanded, 'Do not let me see your faces unless your youngest brother is with you!'"

Jacob shook his head. "No," he said. His voice choked with tears. "I will never let Benjamin go. His brother, Joseph, is dead, and he is the only son of Rachel who is left. If anything happened to him, I could not go on living!"

"Then we cannot go," the brothers said. "Please, father, let me take Benjamin," Judah said. "I promise to bring him back to you."

Jacob stared at the ground. When he raised his head, he spoke slowly and sadly. "Take your

brother Benjamin and return at once to the storehouse in Egypt. Go! And may God watch over you! As for me, if my children are to die, I can do nothing to save them."

So Jacob's sons went down to Egypt for the second time. Once more they stood before Joseph.

Joseph looked quickly from one to the other. Yes, Benjamin was here!

"Take the men into my house," Joseph commanded his servant.

The men were afraid. "This must be a trick," they whispered. "They want to get us into the house so they can attack us and take us as slaves. They'll say we stole the money we found in our bags."

So they spoke to Joseph's servant. "When we opened our bags last time, each of us found his money on top of the grain. We do not know who put it there, but we brought it back to return to you."

The servant looked surprised.

"You owe me nothing," he said. "You gave me your payment the last time."

And he brought their brother Simeon to them. Simeon was safe and well. Then, he brought the men into Joseph's house. He gave them water to bathe their burning feet, and food for their animals.

The brothers had brought many gifts for Joseph. They now laid out their gifts, and waited for Joseph to arrive. When Joseph came home, they gave him the gifts, and bowed low before him.

"How is your old father of whom you spoke?" Joseph asked. "Is he still in good health?"

"He is in good health," they answered. And they bowed low again.

Joseph looked about. "Is this your youngest brother?" he asked, pointing to Benjamin.

Before anyone could answer, Joseph hurried out of the room for he suddenly felt like crying! Alone in another room he burst into tears. Then, he washed his face and went back to the others.

"Serve the meal!" he ordered. At this, a side door opened and servants ran in carrying bowls of steaming hot food. When everything was set, the brothers were shown to their table.

"Place the men where I tell you," Joseph said to one of his servants. And he had them seated in order of their age, from the oldest to the youngest. The brothers looked at each other. There was great wonder in their eyes!

After the meal, Joseph called his servant aside. "Fill the men's bags with food—as much as they can carry," he whispered. "Then take my silver drinking cup and hide it in the bag of Benjamin, the youngest."

Early the next morning, the men left to return to Canaan.

They had not gone far when they heard a

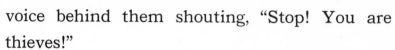
voice behind them shouting, "Stop! You are thieves!"

Looking around, they recognized Joseph's servant.

"Why have you stolen my master's precious drinking cup? How could you do this after he was so good to you?" he said angrily.

"Why do you say such things?" the brothers asked. "None of us has stolen from your master. If you find the cup with one of us, that one shall die, and the rest shall become your slaves."

"No," Joseph's servant said. "Only the one who has the cup will become a slave. The rest will be free."

Without saying any more, each man lowered his bag to the ground and opened it. The servant searched, beginning with the oldest and ending with the youngest. "Here it is!" he called out, as he pulled the cup out of Benjamin's bag.

The brothers could not believe their eyes! "There is surely some mistake," they cried. "We will not let you take our youngest brother. We will *all* go back to your master."

22

"I am Joseph"

When the brothers returned to Joseph's palace, they threw themselves on the ground before him.

"Why did you steal my cup?" Joseph asked angrily.

"Oh, Great Man of Egypt," Judah answered, "how can we prove that we are not thieves? You found the cup in one of our bags, so you cannot believe that we are innocent. But we ask one kindness of you. Take us *all* as your slaves—not just our youngest brother."

"No," Joseph answered. "Only the one in whose bag the cup was found will be my slave. The rest of you may go back to your father."

Then Judah spoke again. "Please listen to me," he said. "If we come home, and Benjamin is not with us, our father will surely die. I beg of you, let *me* stay and be your slave in my brother's place. Send *him* home so that our father may live."

Joseph could no longer keep his secret.

"Leave me alone with these men," he called out to all who were in the room.

When every stranger had gone, Joseph burst into loud sobbing. "I am Joseph!" he cried. His brothers only stared at him.

"I am your brother Joseph—whom you sold into Egypt," he said again.

The brothers still stared. They could not speak or move.

"Do not be afraid," Joseph went on. "And do not be angry with yourselves because you sold me into slavery. It was not *you* who sent me here, but *God*. He sent me here so that I could save your lives and the life of my father when hunger came to the land. God has made me ruler over the whole land of Egypt.

"Now hurry back to Canaan. Tell my father all I have told you. Then bring him, and your families, down to Egypt. You will live near me, in a place called Goshen. I will take good care of you." Then Joseph kissed his brothers and began to cry again.

When Pharaoh heard that Joseph's brothers were in Egypt, he was pleased.

Pharaoh said to Joseph, "Say to your brothers, 'Load your animals with food and return at once to the land of Canaan. Take your father and your wives and children, and bring them here.'"

Then Pharaoh stopped and thought for a moment.

"Say this also to your brothers," he said. "'Take with you, from the land of Egypt, wagons, so that your old father and your families may travel here in comfort. Do not bring your belongings from Canaan. When you come back I will give you everything you need and you will make your home in the best part of Egypt.'"

The brothers did as Pharaoh commanded. They got wagons from Joseph and returned to Canaan. "Joseph is still alive," they said to Jacob. "He is ruler over the whole land of Egypt!" "No," whispered Jacob, not daring to believe them, "that cannot be so."

But when they told him all that Joseph had said to them, and when he saw the wagons that Joseph had sent, he knew it was true!

"My son Joseph is still alive! I will see him before I die," Jacob said. And the sadness went out of his face.

23

No Revenge

Jacob lived seventeen years in Egypt.

When it was almost time for him to die, he called his son Joseph, and said, "You must make me a promise. When I die, take my body back to Canaan, and bury me in the Cave of Machpelah. It is the cave that my grandfather Abraham bought as a burial place for all our family."

"I will do as you have spoken," Joseph said.

After this, Joseph brought his sons Ephraim and Manasseh to visit Jacob. "Let them stand near me so that I may bless them," Jacob said.

The boys walked to the bed and stood beside their grandfather, one at his right and one at his left. Slowly and painfully, Jacob sat up. He placed his hands on his grandsons' heads and blessed them.

"May God, who has been my shepherd from birth unto this day, bless these boys. And may

their children, and those who come after them, always remember my name and the names of my fathers, Abraham and Isaac."

Then came the day of Jacob's death. Joseph and his brothers wept for their father, and carried him back to Canaan, as he had asked. There they buried him in the Cave of Machpelah, in the city of Hebron, as Joseph had promised.

Now that their father was dead, the brothers were afraid. "What if Joseph decides to pay us back now for all the wrong that we did him!" they said.

So they sent Joseph a message saying, "Before your father died, he told us: So shall you say to Joseph, 'I beg you to forgive your brothers who treated you so badly.' "

Joseph listened, and his eyes filled with tears.

Then his brothers came before him and said, "Take us as your slaves." But Joseph said to them, "Do not be afraid. I know you sold me into Egypt because you hated me. But God turned it into a good thing—so that I could save the lives of many people. I have really forgiven you, and I will take care of you and your children."

24

The New Pharaoh

Joseph and his brothers never went back to the land of Canaan. They died in Egypt.

For many years, their children and grandchildren lived peacefully in Egypt. They stayed together in Goshen where Pharaoh had let them make their home. Their numbers grew larger and larger, until Goshen was filled with them.

They were called "Israelites" or "the children of Israel."

One day, a new Pharaoh came to the throne of Egypt. He was a king who did not know about Joseph and all he had done for Egypt. This Pharaoh traveled through the land and saw the Israelites living in Goshen.

"They are not like the Egyptians," he thought. "They are different! They are strangers!" Pharaoh did not trust strangers! The new king said to the Egyptians, "There are too many Israelites in our land. Some day, they may even

decide to join our enemies and fight against us. Let us make them slaves. Then, they will die of hard work and there will not be so many Israelites—and they will not dare to fight us."

And that is how the Israelites became slaves in Egypt.

They made bricks, and built cities, and worked in the fields. Day after day, the sun beat down on their half-naked bodies—and the whips of the Egyptians tore into their tired backs.

"More bricks!" shouted the taskmasters.

"Faster!" screamed the overseers.

But Pharaoh was not satisfied. "There are still too many of them," he grumbled. "Hard work does not kill them."

Then he gave a new command. "Watch the Israelite women carefully," he said to his people, "and whenever a *baby boy* is born to one of them, you are to throw that baby into the Nile river! But let the girls live."

In Goshen, an Israelite named Amram lived with his wife and family. Soon after Pharaoh's command, Jochebed, Amram's wife, gave birth to a baby boy.

For three months, the parents hid their baby from the Egyptians. Nobody saw or heard him. But a day came when they knew that they could no longer keep their secret.

"His voice has grown loud and strong," Amram whispered early one morning. "Soon his crying will be heard outdoors. Before long, somebody will come to take him away. How can we save him?"

Jochebed had no answer. All she could do was cradle her baby in her arms and pray that he would not cry. Back and forth, back and forth, back and forth she rocked, trying to keep the baby still.

"Amram," she said suddenly, "bring me a large wicker basket."

Amram did as his wife asked. He placed the basket on the wooden table in the corner of the dark room.

"Now some pitch," she said.

"I don't understand," Amram started to say.

"You'll soon see," Jochebed told him. "Hurry."

She put the baby down on the bed, and began

to work at the table. She covered the inside of the basket with a layer of pitch. Over the pitch she placed many thicknesses of soft cloth. When this was done, she lifted the sleeping child, and gently laid him in the basket.

Amram watched.

"Why are you doing this?" he asked.

Jochebed began to cry. "I am taking our son to the Nile river," she sobbed. "I will place the basket among the tall grasses that grow in the water along the bank. Perhaps somebody will find the baby and take pity on him."

Then she left the house. Miriam, the baby's sister, went with her mother. "Hide in the bushes, and see what happens to your brother," Jochebed said. Then she walked slowly home.

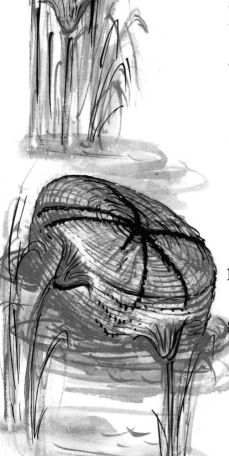

Later that morning, Pharaoh's daughter came down to bathe in the Nile. "What's that?" she asked, pointing to a basket resting among the tall grasses.

"Bring it to me," she said to one of her maidservants. The maidservant stepped forward and picked up the strange-looking basket.

Pharaoh's daughter lifted the lid. "Oh," she gasped, "a baby boy!"

The child began to cry. Pharaoh's daughter

bent over the basket. She touched the baby's soft cheek, and took his small hands into her own.

"This must be an Israelite child," she thought. "Yet, I cannot let him die." The princess stood still, looking down at the basket. She was wondering what to do, when Miriam, the baby's sister, stepped out from her hiding place.

"Perhaps I can help you, your Highness," she said in a trembling voice.

"Help me?" asked the princess, wondering who this little girl was. "How?"

Miriam felt braver now. "Shall I go and call an Israelite woman to take care of this child that you found?"

Pharaoh's daughter smiled at her. "Please do," she said.

Quickly, Miriam ran to find her mother. And Jochebed went with Pharaoh's daughter and became her own baby's nurse.

25

Moses, the Helper

When the little boy grew older, his mother brought him back to Pharaoh's daughter,

"He is *my* son now," the princess said. "I will take good care of him." And she named the boy Moses.

Moses lived in the palace of Pharaoh's daughter. She called him her son, and she loved him very much.

Somehow, Moses found out that he came from the slave people.

One day, when he had grown to be a man, Moses went out to watch the Israelites work. In one place, he saw an Egyptian beating an Israelite.

Moses began to shake with anger!

He looked this way and that. Nobody was about. He hit the Egyptian *with all his strength!* The Egyptian fell at Moses' feet. He was dead!

For a few moments, Moses did not move. He stood and stared down at the man he had killed. Then he hid the dead man in the sand, and left the place.

But even after this, Moses did not stay away from the slaves. He went out again the very next day.

As he stood once more near a group of Israelites at work, Moses suddenly heard the sound of angry voices. He turned and saw two slaves fighting.

"Why do you hit this man?" Moses asked the one who had attacked the other. "Is he not a slave like you?"

At this, the first slave spun around. "Who made you chief over us? Do you mean to kill me like you killed the Egyptian?" he screamed at Moses.

Now Moses was frightened. "People know what happened," he said to himself. "I am not safe in Egypt."

When Pharaoh found out what Moses had done, he tried to have him killed. But Moses learned of the king's plan, and escaped from Egypt.

He walked through the desert, until he reached

a place called Midian. Here, he sat down beside a well to rest.

It was not long before he saw seven shepherdesses walking toward the well. They had come to draw water for their sheep. But no sooner did they lower their buckets than a group of shepherds chased them off. Moses jumped up. "Stop," he shouted at the shepherds. Then he helped the girls water their sheep.

When the shepherdesses returned home, their father, Jethro, was surprised to see them. "How is it that you have come back so soon today?" he asked.

"An Egyptian saved us from the shepherds," the girls answered. "He also drew water for us and watered the flocks."

"Where is he then?" their father asked. "Go and ask him to come and eat with us."

So Moses, the stranger, went with them to their home.

After the meal, Moses told Jethro about the slaves and about killing the Egyptian. He also told him about his escape from Pharaoh.

Jethro listened to every word. He liked the gentle man from Egypt. He said, "You are welcome to stay here with us."

Moses thanked Jethro, and agreed to make his home in Midian.

At last Moses felt at peace. He became a shepherd for Jethro's flocks.

He loved the quiet days out in the fields. And he loved his new home and family. Before long, he married Zipporah, one of Jethro's daughters.

26

The Burning Bush

One pleasant day, Moses was walking along beside the animals. He felt safe and happy. He was not thinking of anything special.

All of a sudden, he stopped and looked around. Where was he? His feet had taken him to a place he had never seen before.

In front of him was a tall mountain—and nearby a bush was on fire. It burned and burned, but did not burn up!

"I must turn aside to look at this wonderful sight," Moses said. "Why is the bush not burned?"

And then he knew!

"Moses, Moses," a voice spoke to him from out of the bush, "the time has come for you to go back to Egypt. You must go to Pharaoh and tell him to let My people, the Israelites, go free!"

"O God," Moses whispered, "who am I that I should go to Pharaoh? Who am I to bring the Israelites out of Egypt?"

"But you *must* go, Moses! I will help you."

"No, no," Moses cried. "I speak slowly and my words are hard to understand. Please send somebody else."

God became angry with Moses. He said, "Your brother Aaron speaks well. He is coming to meet you and he will be happy to help you. You will tell him what to say, and he will speak for you."

Now Moses knew he had to go back. That evening, Moses talked with Jethro. "Let me return to my people in Egypt. I want to see what has been happening to them." Jethro agreed. "Go in peace," he said. (By this time, all who had planned to kill Moses were dead.)

So Moses left the home that he loved, and went back to the land of Egypt. On the way, he met his brother Aaron. Moses told Aaron all that had happened to him near the mountain and the bush.

When they returned to Egypt, Moses and Aaron gathered the Israelite elders. Aaron then told them what God had said to Moses. The people believed them. Then Moses and Aaron went and stood before Pharaoh. "Oh Pharaoh," they said, "the time has come to let the Israelite slaves go out of Egypt. God has said to us, 'Tell Pharaoh to let My people go.'"

But Pharaoh only laughed at them. "I do not know this God of whom you speak, nor will I let the Israelites go," he said. "They will make my bricks and build my cities. They will never leave this land!"

That very day, Pharaoh called together the taskmasters and overseers of the slaves and said, "You shall no longer bring the Israelites the straw they need for mixing into their bricks. From now on, let them go and gather straw *themselves*. But they must keep making the same number of bricks each day that they made until now! They are lazy and do not want to work!"

Now the slaves spent much time looking for straw. On a day when the straw was hard to find and they could not make as many bricks as Pharaoh wanted, life was very hard. Then they were beaten with whips by the Egyptian task-masters.

"O God, won't this ever end?" they cried.

"God will free you from the Egyptians!" Moses promised his people.

But the people could not believe this any longer. "May God punish *you* for going to Pharaoh and bringing new troubles upon us," they said to Moses.

Then Moses called out to God, "Why did You bring harm upon this people? Ever since I came to Pharaoh to say, 'Let the Israelites go,' things have gotten worse for them."

God answered Moses, saying, "Be patient. Soon I will bring great troubles *upon Pharaoh and his people. Then* he will let the Israelites go."

27

The Ten Plagues

For the second time, Moses and Aaron came before Pharaoh. "Let the Israelites go," they said. "Let them go! For if you do not, you will surely be punished by God."

But Pharaoh only laughed again, and he made the slaves work harder than ever.

And then, terrible things began to happen in Egypt. The water of the Nile turned into blood. The land was filled with frogs. The houses were filled with insects.

"God is punishing the Egyptians," Moses said. Pharaoh was afraid.

"Call Moses and Aaron," he commanded. "I am ready to let the Israelites go," he said, when Moses and Aaron reached the palace.

But soon Pharaoh changed his mind. "No, no, no!" he screamed, "I shall never let them go!"

More and more strange and frightening things happened in Egypt. Again and again, Pharaoh

said, "Yes, I will let the Israelites go!" and then, "No, I have changed my mind!"

But, at last, he stopped changing his mind.

God had sent ten terrible troubles—ten plagues—to Egypt. Pharaoh and his people were tired and worried.

"Moses, take your Israelites and leave this land at once," Pharaoh ordered.

"Hurry. Take your people away," the Egyptians cried. "If the Israelites stay any longer, we shall all be dead."

Then Moses spoke to the Israelites. "Gather your belongings, and prepare to leave this land quickly," he said to them. "Pharaoh is sending us out of Egypt!"

Hardly knowing what they were doing, the people packed their few belongings. "Hurry, hurry," the Egyptians kept saying. "Take what you have and go!" And the slaves hurried. So much did they hurry, that they did not even have time to bake bread to eat on the way. Instead, those who had prepared dough for baking, wrapped it carefully in cloths, and carried it on their shoulders.

Then, the long walk out of Egypt began. Moses led the way, and behind him came the

Israelites—men, women, and children—all who had once been slaves.

After a few hours, the Israelites came to their first resting place.

One by one, the women lowered the precious bread-dough from their shoulders—the dough they had carried out of Egypt. They made ovens out of the hot desert stones and prepared to bake their bread.

Imagine their disappointment when they unwrapped the dough and saw that it had not risen! It was flat—not high and puffy as bread-dough should be. But they had no other food, so they put the flat dough into the ovens and waited.

The dough baked quickly. But instead of turning into bread, it turned into something flat and hard—much like the *matzot* we have today.

The Israelites ate these *matzot* hungrily. They were happy to have food. Then Moses said to them, "You must always remember this day on which God set you free from Egypt. And this is what you must do to help you remember:

"Every year, when it is spring time, as it is now, you will make a holiday for seven days. On these seven days, there must be no bread in your houses. You will eat only *matzot*. And when your children ask, 'Why do we celebrate this holiday?' you shall answer them: 'Because we want to remember that once we were slaves in Egypt, and then God set us free.' "

When Pharaoh heard that the Israelites were gone, he suddenly had a change of heart.

"What fools we were to set the slaves free," he said. "Who will work in our cities and care for our fields? Come, let us chase after them and bring them back!"

Pharaoh's officers did as the king commanded. They took all the chariots of Egypt and the chariot horses, and rode after the Israelite slaves.

The Israelites were camped near a place named the Sea of Reeds. As Pharaoh's armies drew near, the Israelites noticed them.

"Moses, why did you bring us here?" they cried out. "Did we not say to you in Egypt, 'Leave us alone. It is better to be slaves for Pharaoh than to die in the wilderness?' "

"Do not be afraid," Moses answered the people. "God will protect you from Pharaoh."

Then a strong wind began to blow from the east. It blew against the sea and split the water in two. It pushed the waters aside until a path

formed across the sea. And the Israelites stepped onto the path and walked between two walls of water until they reached the opposite shore.

"After them!" shouted the Egyptian officers. And they, too, went into the sea.

"Faster, faster!" they yelled, as they whipped their horses to make them run.

But Pharaoh's chariots could not move quickly on the wet sea floor. Their wheels sank deep into the muddy bottom until they could no longer turn.

"We cannot get across," the Egyptian officers called to their men. "Let us return to the shore."

The horsemen tried to turn their chariots around. But it was too late! The walls of water that stood on either side of the dry path tumbled back to their place and threw the Egyptians into the sea. Not one of them was saved.

28

God Teaches the Israelites

Three months after leaving Egypt, the Israelites stopped near a mountain. It was called Mount Sinai. Here they made their camp.

Early on the morning of the third day great bursts of thunder and lightning shook Mount Sinai. Thick clouds covered the mountain, and the sound of a giant horn was heard. The people shook with fear.

Then Moses led the Israelites out of the camp, and together they stood at the foot of Mount Sinai. As they watched, the whole mountain began to tremble, and thick, black smoke poured forth from its top. The noise of the horn grew louder and louder; lightning tore through the sky; thunder rumbled with a deafening sound.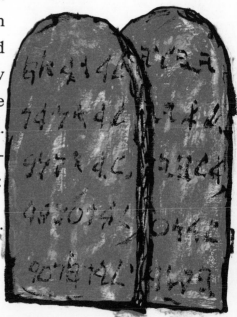

Then God began to speak. The people listened as He taught them Ten Commandments:

1. I am God who brought you out of Egypt. You must have no other gods besides me.

2. You must not bow down to any statues and call them gods.

3. You must not say the name God, except at important times.

4. Set aside the Sabbath day. Neither you, nor your animals, nor anyone who lives with you must do work on the Sabbath.

5. Honor your father and your mother.

6. You shall not murder.

7. You shall not take away another person's husband or wife.

8. You shall not steal.

9. You shall not tell lies about your neighbor.

10. You shall not want your neighbor's house, nor anything else that belongs to him.

The people moved back from the mountain.

"Moses," they said, "*you* tell us what God wants, and we will obey. But do not let God speak to us any more, for we are afraid that we will die."

So Moses became the teacher of the people.

Later, Moses taught the Israelites the other laws of God—the things God wanted them to do.

Some of these laws were:

—Treat a stranger kindly. Do not hurt him. Remember how the Egyptians treated you because you were strangers, and do not do the same to other people.

—Help the poor, and anyone else who needs your help.

—When you harvest your grain, do not cut the grain that grows in the corners of your fields. That belongs to the poor. They will come and gather it so they may have food.

These laws and commandments were written down in the Torah—and the Jewish people still read them and learn from them today.

For forty long years, Moses and the Israelites traveled in the wilderness, on their way to the land of Canaan, where Abraham, Isaac, and Jacob had once lived.

Sometimes, the people felt happy. "It is good to be free," they thought to themselves.

But other times, they were afraid. "Where will we find food? How will we get water?"

They complained to Moses saying, "It was better in Egypt. Why did you bring us here? We shall starve to death!"

"God will help you," Moses answered patiently.

And he was right! The people found food to eat and water to drink in the wilderness!

At last, the forty years passed and the journey of the Israelites was almost over. One bright day, Moses and the people stood beside the Jordan river. The land of Canaan could be seen on the other shore. Moses spoke:

"Hear, O Israel!

"You are about to cross the Jordan into the land of Canaan—the land of Abraham, Isaac, and Jacob.

"When you come to that land, you must not forget the things that you learned in the wilderness.

"Remember the Ten Commandments, and the other laws that you learned here.

"Teach them to your children. And tell them to teach them to *their* children. For these are the things God wants of us."

Now, Moses knew that it was time for him to die.

He had lived to be very old, and had done many great things in his lifetime. He had known much sadness, and also much happiness.

But one happiness could not be his. He was never to go into the land of Canaan!

Sadly, Moses blessed his people. Then he climbed to the top of a tall mountain that stood beside the Jordan river. From here, he looked across at the land on which his feet would never stand.

And here, the great teacher, Moses, died.